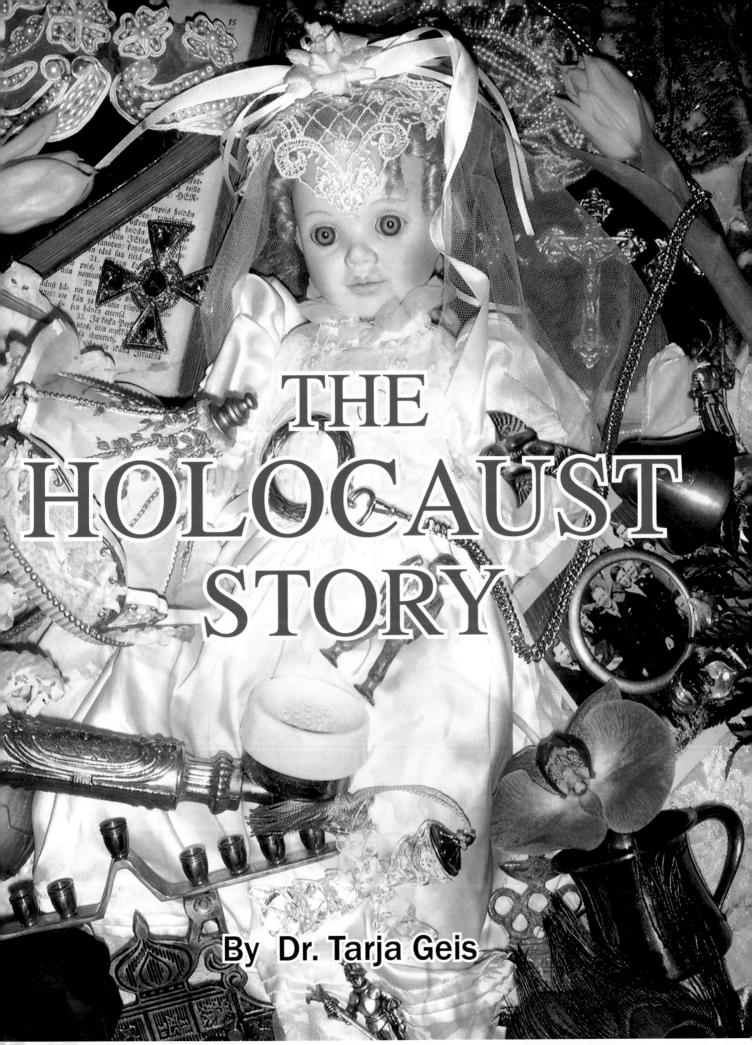

DEDICATION

The Holocaust Story is dedicated and devoted to all present and bygone victims of prejudice, bias, disability, racism, war, poverty, illness, hatred, bullying, and harassment.

May a light in their hearts and a warming love bring comfort and a radiance extinguishing persecution. May the illumination of love and peace prevail.

To order additional copies of this book, contact:
Xlibris
1-888-795-4274
www.Xlibris.com
Orders@Xlibris.com

ISBN: Softcover   978-1-4257-3469-5
        Ebook   978-1-9845-8410-6

Print information available on the last page

Rev. date: 07/31/2020

INTRODUCTION

This story was written as an introduction to the Holocaust. It is appropriate for very young children, or for anyone wanting to learn about this period in history. The writing and illustrations are very simple and straightforward. It was written to introduce and enhance the understanding of the Holocaust. We all learn lessons from mistakes. There are many lessons to learn from this terrible period in history. May the world never again experience the horrors of World War II or other horrific events like African American slavery.

Children of today are the leaders of tomorrow. They need knowledge of the past. This world will be theirs. Our children today will be the leaders making choices for us in our tomorrows. May their innocence, love, knowledge, and understanding guide the future. They are born without prejudice and without hate. Our children are the hope of the world.

Many years ago, much fighting and anger took place.
This time was called World War Two (WWII, 1939-1945).

Terrible things happened because countries and people wanted power and were hurting others to get more and more land and power.

Armies in Europe, Africa, and Asia, fought and fought. Pearl Harbor in Hawaii was attacked. A huge bomb was dropped on Japan. Many people were hurt. Many people died. Buildings and cities were destroyed.

A leader in Germany named Adolf Hitler (dictator) gained greater and greater power. He told many lies (propaganda) and people believed him and followed him.

Hitler only liked people who were like him (prejudice). He blamed (scapegoat) the Jewish people for the poor conditions in Germany.

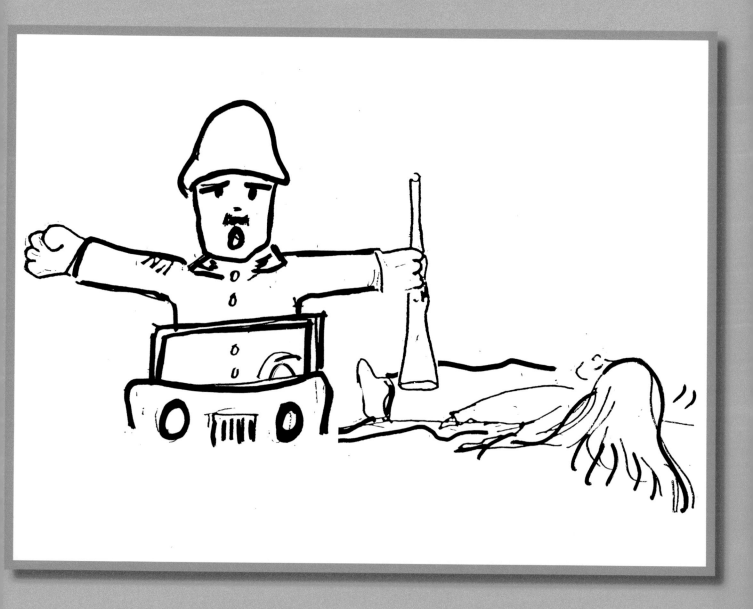

Hitler was a powerful, angry man who began hurting
(persecuting) (bullying) many innocent people (victims).
He started to capture and kill (genocide) all of the Jewish
families and anyone who did not obey him and his laws.

Hitler's armies and followers were mean and told lies. They sent people they didn't like to concentration camps.

These people lost everything they owned...their clothes, their books, their homes, their money, their jobs, and their food. Families were pulled apart. They were taken from the people they loved. It was a terrible time.

Sometimes the victims would hide in the forests, in caves, and barns. Some people tried to help. They gave food and safety to these victims. They (rescuers) tried to get them to safe lands (refugees), away from Hitler's Nazi soldiers.

People were scared and frightened. Many were afraid to help (bystanders).

Some people pretended nothing bad was going on.
Others were fighting their own wars and didn't help.

Other people resisted and said, "NO!" Many gave up and some didn't care.

By the end of WWII, Hitler's armies and followers had killed millions and millions of people. The people of the world were sad when they realized what terrible things happened. The people in the concentration camps were freed (liberated) and became the survivors of the Holocaust.

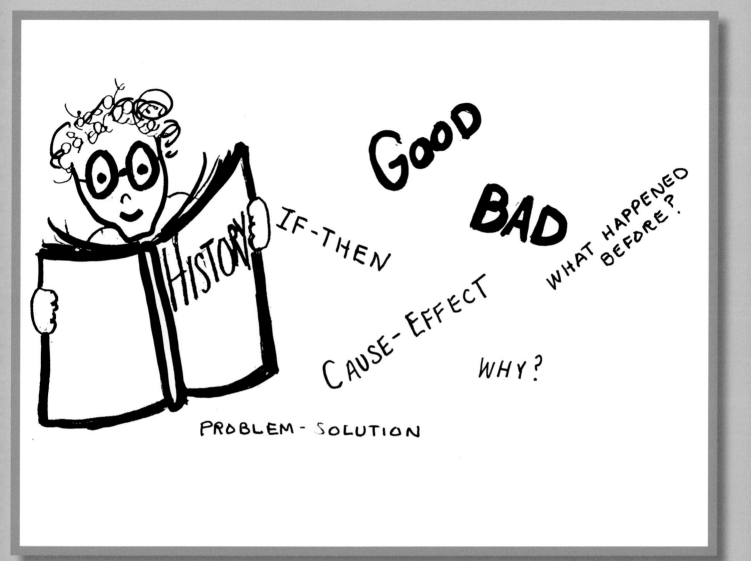

We will never let such a horrible event happen again. We study history and the Holocaust to learn about the mistakes that have happened in the past. There are many things from history that are good and we learn from those also.

When we see something bad, we must say "NO!" We can make a difference.

We learn from the past. Learn to problem solve today.
Learn to become good world citizens for tomorrow. We
are the future of the world. We must honor others
equally with LOVE, PEACE, and GOOD WILL.

Learning about terrible times in the past like the Holocaust and African American slavery are lessons for all of us.

Today, we learn from these lessons. We know events like the Holocaust were horrible and wrong. We need to respect all cultures, help all people, and celebrate diversity and our differences.

HOPE
Dr. Tarja Geis

Judge me not by my
    Color,
    Heritage,
    Nationality,
    Or Creed.
For I am not my
    Grandfather,
    Mother,
    Great Uncle,
    Or Relation.
Blame me not for
    Atrocities,
    Slavery,
    The Holocaust,
    Prejudice,
    Or Hatred.
For I am
    Fresh,
    Innocent,
    Loving,
    Tranquil,
    And Hopeful.
I am a child.
I am the future.

BLAME ME NOT
By Dr. Tarja Anneli Pelto Geis

Blame me not for the horrors of
Slavery, the Holocaust, and wars.

I am not of the past.
I am a child.

Blame me not
For the mistakes of my ancestors.

Teach me history without bias.
So, I will not repeat mistakes.

Allow me to judge, act, and decide.
View me with optimism and love.

I am the future.
I am a child.

I am HOPE.

WHISPERS

I am a child!
I am a child!
Does no one understand?
I should be nourished, taken care of,
Loved,
Not pushed, hushed, beaten,
Experimented upon,
And forced to labor.
I cry silent tears.
Afraid to sound for fear.
A fear of dying.
A fear of another beating.
My strength is gone.
I merely exist.
A creature fending for survival.
Filth, stench, silence.
My childhood forsaken.
Forced to exist in this horror.
My memories of love,
The joys of family,
Keep a flutter of hope alive.
Deep inside,
Silent.
Silent.

SLIVERS OF HOPE

Slivers of hope amongst the
Abundance of despair.
Miniscule yearnings between the
Moments of sleep, deep into the night.
No food for this dying body.
No life to maintain this soul.
Exhaustion, humiliation.

The essence of my being,
But a flickering flame,
Fighting against the wind.

MEMORIES
OF THE
PAST

WE SHAPE OUR WORLD

WE HAVE THE SAME FUNDAMENTAL NEEDS FOR

SURVIVAL, FUFILLMENT, LOVE, AND SUCCESS

OUR FUTURE DEPENDS ON WORLDWIDE CITIZENSHIP

DEVELOP A GLOBAL VISION

NURTURE THE EARTH AND ITS CHILDREN

INDEX

FOLLOW UP

Suggestions for teachers, counselors, and parents for discussion
and assignments.
The Holocaust Story is adaptable to all levels and areas of curriculum. It can be
adapted to numerous content and skill objectives.

Cause...Effect   Solutions....Alternatives (Good? Bad?)
If...then   Author's Purpose
Emotions...Feelings   Illustrations Poems Prompts Writing
What would you do if_____?
Webbing   Brainstorming   Mapping Skills.....Locating Countries
Population Comparisons (11 million deaths)
Current Events...Current Wars and Genocides   Timelines (Real life math)
Core Values: Cooperation, Fairness, Integrity, Citizenship, Responsibility...etc.
Nutrition   Compare and Contrast   Vocabulary Development
Acting Out Drama   Dialogue   Comparisons to Own Life
Research: Internet, Personal, Media, Interview
Main Idea   Details   Author's Purpose
Health   Survival   Human Needs
Worldwide Governments, Leaders, and Organizations
Music and Art of the Era   Religion   Beliefs   Comparisons
Technology and Scientific Discoveries and Impacts
Pen...E-Mail Pals...Visits (web or personal) to Holocaust Museums
What If...The Technology and Communication of Today Existed in 1942?
Historical Impacts and Lessons From the Past
Pretend You Are a News Reporter   Write an Obituary or Editorial
What Can This Period in History Teach Us as Worldwide Citizens?

QUICK AND EASY
BRAIN COMPATIBLE
HANDS ON PROJECTS
FOLLOWING...

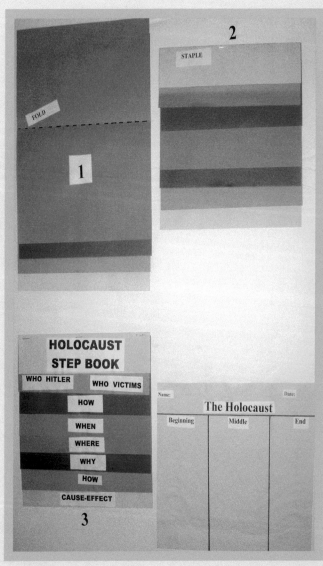

Printed in the United States
By Bookmasters